M000207313

Foxhead Books

Portland | Tipp City | Palo Alto

THE LITTLE BOOK OF TERROR

BY DAISY ROCKWELL

Library of Congress Data

Rockwell, Anne Daisy.

The Little Book of Terror / Anne Daisy Rockwell—1st Ed.

84 pages. .95 cm.

ISBN 13 978-0-9847486-1-7

ISBN 10 098474861X

1. Non-Fiction—Essays. 2. Non-Fiction—Politics. 3. Non-Fiction—History. 4. Art—Painters—Lapata.

Cover image: "Couple" © 2010 Anne Daisy Rockwell.

For my father

Contents

Foreword

by Amitava Kumar

Amitava Kumar

Self Radicalized Woman With Small Stuffed Bear.

A terrorist has a hard life. You might be a wanted man (or, more rarely, woman), and yet, your pictures on the FBI's website show you in a state of unkempt disregard.

Your grainy photo appears under large, unattractive type, and the picture itself is nothing to boast about: you are unshaven and look disoriented, you appear in need of a hot breakfast, and, the worst indignity of all, the lighting always sucks. The State, in other words, is a makeup artist.

In the long-running soap opera called the 'War on Terror' (Ten Successful Seasons—And Still Going Strong! We have touched more lives worldwide than any other show!! The New York Times has dubbed it 'The Bomb'!!!), the terrorists are the shabbiest actors ever to flit across our screens. They have the worst lines and meet bad ends, of course, but their photos also reveal the State's skill at presenting us people who come to us stripped of any sign of place or a past.

In contrast, I think of Daisy Rockwell's portraits of terrorists as a bright, playful gallery composed of pictures that the terrorists themselves might put up on their Facebook pages.

Consider one of my favorite Rockwell paintings called 'Tuna Princess.' A young man with black, dreamy eyes lolls on his stomach on a large bed with a floral bedcover. He is cuddling a black cat. The cat and the young man are both gazing at us. They seem to be calmly, even cautiously, assessing our look. The caption reads:

'Mohamed Mahmood Alessa was arrested with his friend (and co-conspirator) on the way to join a militant group in Somalia. His mother has said that he wanted to take his cat, Tuna Princess, with him, but she did not allow it and they argued. Eventually he left instead with a large bag of candy from his parents' deli. The candy was seized by the FBI.'

What has happened here? Why is Rockwell, as Sarah Palin might put it, palling around with terrorists?

I have long held that many of the writers and artists working in the aftermath of the September 11 attacks have presented a faux familiarity with the so-called terrorist mind.

Rockwell's art makes no such claims. It returns us to what is real—and therefore surprising—about human lives. She has painted portraits of Osama bin Laden and Mullah Omar, and there must be some bravery involved in putting these up on the walls of a gallery, but what she is especially good at is painting those one would call ordinary terrorists.

These are people who might be behind bars but in the paintings emerge as individuals who are neither particularly heroic nor particularly villainous. This isn't what Don DeLillo was writing about in a recent short-story *Baader Meinhof* that invoked the art of Gerhard Richter—I don't believe Rockwell is interested in convincing a viewer that even terrorists can be forgiven. There is too much irony in her paintings, and often, also glitter.

Rockwell leaves easy moralism to the law-makers and the law-breakers. There is ambiguity in her art, and, more than that, a plain sense of attention. It is as if in an effort to find more about the world in which we are living, a world where the war on terror is a fact, the artist has finally found a human face.

A further remark can be made: where the FBI image represses drama—and therefore life—Rockwell seems to revel in it.

In this respect, her paintings resemble the old Bollywood posters hand-painted by artists with a keen sense of the fantastic. The hero, the heroine, the villain, all painted in lurid colors of the imagination! Against the miserliness of the moralizers, you here have the wit and exuberance of the inventive artist.

In fact, Rockwell the painter is so far from the pundits that she has happily painted the aforementioned Ms. Palin too, wearing red shoes, seated on a sofa, surrounded by dead animals. The politicians in the news, stranded on the remote hills of rhetoric, are reduced to physical objects in Rockwell's small paintings.

There are portraits of the Ayatollah as a loveable scamp or frolicking in a purple forest. Barack Obama, as a boy, standing on the tarmac, his father's arms around him. There is also Putin, bare-chested, riding a horse, or, in another one, patting a tiger at his feet.

I like to think that these are the portraits that Putin might put on his Facebook page. Long before Facebook, Rockwell's famous grandfather, the artist Norman Rockwell, was painting extraordinary pictures of ordinary people.

In 1963, the year of my birth, he painted a work called 'The Problem We All Live With,' depicting Ruby Bridges, the six-year-old girl who was the first African-American child to attend an all-white elementary school in the South. Norman Rockwell's painting shows the solitary girl's march to school while flanked by U.S. Marshals. On the wall behind her we can see scrawled a racist slur.

On a warm summer day, I drove to North Adams to be present at the opening of an exhibition of paintings by Daisy Rockwell; enroute, I stopped at the Norman Rockwell Museum in Stockbridge, Massachusetts.

There, I saw 'The Problem We All Live With,' which is now on loan to the White House. There were many familiar works that I recognized on the museum's walls but one that drew my attention was an oil-painting titled 'The Peace Corps in India.'

Painted in 1966, it showed a young woman, with short, blond hair, leaning over a desk on which were arranged small rock samples being examined by six Indian boys in white shirts. Rockwell's painting was an illustration for *Look*.

A plaque on the wall said:

'For his painting about education in India, Rockwell relied on his impressions of the country from an earlier trip. 'The Peace Corps only teaches among the high school age Indian,' he explained in a letter to his editor, 'I have the kids working on mineralogy.' Rockwell included the government's seal of three lions, as he had seen on a school in New Delhi.'

As I stood looking at the painting, I thought of Daisy Rockwell. Unlike her grandfather, unlike the Peace Corps teacher, Rockwell's engagement with the subcontinent has been deeper and more thorough.

She earned a PhD in Hindi literature from the University of Chicago; her book on the Hindi writer Upendranath Ashk wonderfully evokes both the man and his milieu. Rockwell's writing about Ashk actually becomes a biography of Hindi literature.

The immersion in a large body of literature means that Rockwell makes startling discoveries. At one point, she notes that unlike many novels written by South Asians about the subcontinent, there is barely any mention in Hindi writing about poor sanitation or strong smells.

Rockwell writes that because 'poor sanitation and strong smells are mundane aspects of India's everyday environment, they are not considered worth mentioning,' and, furthermore, 'the audience for Hindi literature is primarily Indian, and therefore, it does not need to be told what it already knows.'

This is revealing. It offers us a way of looking with fresh eyes at the paintings in this book. I don't only have in mind Rockwell's witty caption for the painting of the so-called American Taliban:

'John Walker Lindh is the ultimate foreign exchange student. He left the U.S. to study Arabic and ended up training with al Qaeda in Afghanistan. His Arabic is reportedly good.'

Rather, I'm thinking more visually, particularly of what Rockwell chooses to put in her pictures of someone like Ilyas Kashmiri. The news-reports had said that the terrorist had been killed in a U.S. drone attack while he sat taking tea in an apple orchard.

In Rockwell's portrait, we see a nearly ethereal apple tree in the center, with a full canopy of gleaming apples. On the left, lying on the ground, is Kashmiri's severed head, his glasses still magically intact on his head; on the right, to counterbalance the head that is gushing blood, there is a green teapot and the pretty tea-cup from which tea has spilled.

Too late now for Kashmiri to choose an image for his Facebook page, but I see the appeal of an art whose status update is that it rebuilds devastated landscapes, restoring to them shatter-proof eyeglasses, bomb-defying apple trees, and the peace-loving gesture of pouring tea into pretty tea-cups.

I.

Why Do They Hate Us?

Daisy's friend, the blogger Sepoy, grew a beard. This inspired a series of portraits based on the nine traditional Indian rasas, or emotional states, delineated by ancient Sanskrit aestheticians. This one is the rasa of fear.

Early in the morning on September 11, 2001, I spoke on the phone with a student of mine. After briefly discussing the attacks on the World Trade Center, which had just occurred, he asked, half joking, 'will you come visit me at the concentration camp?' He was referring to his religion (Muslim by birth) and his skin color (brown).

A couple days later, a group of female students came to my office. They all wore hijab and were anxious because, they said, their fathers had told them not to wear any head coverings for the time being in order to avoid hate crimes. They had previously understood their commitment to wearing hijab as an act of pride in their faith that should not be abandoned in the face of ignorance or hate. But should they ignore their fathers?

They did.

This one is anger.

Around that same time I went to discuss the logistics of a teach-in about the crisis with the dean of the college where I taught.

'Have you heard,' he asked in a hushed voice, 'that there was cheering in the dorms?'

'Pardon me?' I asked.

Somehow he managed to indicate to me in a circuitous manner that he was referring to the Muslim students whose families were from India and Pakistan, many of whom were in my classes on Hindi-Urdu and South Asian literature.

He had heard, he told me, that some students had been cheering as the attacks had occurred.

'No,' I replied evenly, 'I had not heard that.'

I added that the prevailing mood was one of fear; fear of being attacked for their religion or ethnicity; fear of having their civil liberties curtailed for those same reasons.

I wondered if his question originated from his own paranoia, or if law enforcement officials had already been by to plant the seeds of suspicion.

This one is humor.

In the years immediately following the attacks, the notion that Americans were having trouble processing the attacks had strong currency in the media.

A 'failure of imagination' was often cited. In the classrooms where I stood, there was no such failure. From the earliest moments of al Qaeda's immensely successful operation, anyone with a knowledge of the histories of empires in general and an awareness of the geopolitical goals of the U.S. government, in particular, could comprehend the motivations behind the attacks and could guess what would come next from our president.

The immediate suspicion toward all persons of Muslim background, regardless of their actual beliefs, practices or citizenship was expected because it was already on its way. Curtailment of civil liberties for Muslims under suspicion was clearly prefigured in the treatment of Japanese Americans during World War II.

This time, though, there have been no concentration camps, just bizarre plots, often hatched by the FBI itself, indefinite detentions, fear-mongering trials and lots and lots of spying.

And here is heroic.

The tenth anniversary of the attacks on 9/11 came sandwiched between two highly publicized surprise attacks by the United States.

The first was the commando raid and assassination of Osama bin Laden in his hide-out in Abbottabad, in which the supposed mastermind of the 9/11 attacks was executed without trial following an invasion into sovereign Pakistani airspace by a contingent of U.S. Navy Seals.

The second was the extrajudicial execution of Anwar al-Awlaki, a U.S. citizen, in Yemen, by drone strike. The execution of bin Laden could be seen as an act of war, in retaliation for the attacks on U.S. soil.

But how do we frame the execution of al-Awlaki, an American citizen?

And this one is peaceful.

Why do they hate us, indeed.

And who are they?

And who are we?

II.

Blood Lust

Osama bin Laden death mask.

After watching *Gone with the Wind* at an impressionable age, I became obsessed with the flexibility of Clark Gable's eyebrows.

I endeavored for many months afterwards to develop the muscles necessary to produce similar effects with my own eyebrows.

I now bear the mark of my success on my 42-year-old-face: a surprising fountain of wrinkles originating from my left eyebrow and shooting upward toward my hairline that seem to have materialized overnight. At night, brushing my teeth before the mirror, I stare intently at the wrinkles and try to produce the facial expressions that created them.

And then, I naturally think about age, and about death, and about Osama bin Laden's face, and what, exactly, the Navy Seals did to it that makes photographs of his face unfit for public consumption.

Taliban leader Mullah Omar continues to enjoy a pastoral existence somewhere in Afghanistan or Pakistan, despite the drones' best efforts.

Whenever an impossibly famous individual disappears without a public viewing of the body (and sometimes even then; cf: Elvis), rumors abound as to whether the personage in question is actually dead.

The curious decision to keep from the public the image that would prove the kill has naturally fueled an abundance of theories. So that members of the U.S. government might not also feel inclined to indulge in such conspiracy theorizing, the White House set up a limited access peep-show to which select individuals of prominent stature, such as John McCain, were invited to see the booty captured and killed by our boys.

They came away convinced, slightly shaken, perhaps a little horrified, but gratified that with their tremendous stature came access to the nation's top-drawer death porn.

Saddam Hussein was rooted out 'like a rat in a hole'.

Were his brains blown out? His eyes shot from his head? And if his face was revoltingly disfigured, how then would such a photograph make indisputable his identity in death?

What vestige of his face was left to prove to John McCain with a photo that we had our man? With the capture of Saddam Hussein, the captors chose to distribute a humiliating image of the former leader sticking his head out of his foxhole, groggy, ungroomed, a wild-eyed old man blinking in the sudden light of the sun.

'He was in the bottom of a hole with no way to fight back,' reported Major General Raymond Odierno proudly. 'He was caught like a rat.'

The photograph was depressing as it was convincing, and in any event, he was executed eventually. Blood lust satisfied, conspiracy theories crushed (unless it was one of his doubles?).

Pakistani militant Ilyas Kashmiri was allegedly killed by drone strike, while taking his tea in an orchard.

In Osama's case, at least, there is said to be a photo, and there is said to have been a body, now swimming with the fishes off the coast of Karachi.

In the case of the alleged killing of Pakistani militant Ilyas Kashmiri by drone in 2011, there seems no way of proving the deed. As Interior Minister Rehman Malik put it, officials were '98% sure' that Kashmiri was one of the humans blown up by the drone.

The target was said to be taking his tea in an orchard at the time, an image that bears with it a fragile, civilized gentility in comparison with the CIA's not particularly covert video game-like military operation in Pakistan. Soon after he was supposedly killed, Kashmiri's family gave an almost irritable interview that seemed rather pointed in its criticism of the missing father and husband: he doesn't call, he doesn't write; if you are reading this right now, Ilyas K, you should know that your family is not pleased with your behavior.

They said they'd believe he was dead when they had proof. Of course they'll never have it; the United States has become too fastidious to parade its victims' heads in the village square.

III.

The Best of All Possible Care

Charles Granier and Lynndie England, Abu Ghraib torturers,
enjoy a pleasant moment.

One thing that the First World really gets right is good dental care. The more money you have, the better your teeth. Unfortunately, despite the fact that we Americans (those with dental insurance) have some of the pearliest, straightest teeth in the world, we are seldom grateful. The word 'torture' is probably used far more by Americans to describe visits to the dentist, the periodontist, the orthodontist and the oral surgeon than it is to describe waterboarding or taking photographs of prisoners of war in humiliating poses. That's why the U.S. government is so crafty when it shows us images of bad guys in captivity receiving dental care. Take, for example, José Padilla: the so-called 'dirty bomb' maker was shown in a small video being marched down the hall from his solitary confinement to get a root canal (wearing goggles and sound-canceling headphones to keep that solitary real). This little bit of film was so noteworthy that it was even discussed by Graham Bader in *Artforum*, according to Amitava Kumar, who writes:

> Bader's point is that the most intensely politicized contemporary images are those that concern 'the state's role in authoring the most basic experiences of life and death.' Images like those of 'the broken figure of Jose Padilla, shuffling to the dentist down the hall from his cell' enter our conversations about art as new evidence to be examined and understood.

Having not, in fact, read the original *Artforum* article, I confess that I am flummoxed as to how the video managed to pass directly from the hands of Homeland Security (or the CIA?) directly into the pages of one of the nation's leading art journals. It's so hard to keep track of what is art nowadays.

Former Iraqi premier Saddam Hussein receives top-notch dental care.

This description reminded me of one of my personal favorites in GWOT imagery, specifically from the Iraq war: the photographs of Saddam Hussein receiving the best of all possible medical care at the hands of the U.S. military after he was dragged out of his hiding spot and taken into custody.

It's one of those pieces of propaganda that makes it hard to decide whether you are looking at a really clever piece of psy-ops or an elaborate visual gag. How civilized, and how supremely humane of the United States, to supply that bastard Saddam ('Sadly Insane' as I once heard a caller refer to him on the radio back in the heyday of the Iraq war) with the best possible dental care in the world!

And yet, when Americans see the picture, they know what's really going on: they've sent the dentists in; he's being tortured.

IV.

Little Green Men

Tennessee resident Gary Middleton worries that the mosque could house extremists. 'It's just another mosque, training kids to be terrorist,' he said.

Stan Whiteway also objects to a new mosque for local Muslims. 'I'm sorry, but they seem to be against everything that I believe in. So I don't want them necessarily in my neighborhood,' he said.

—From an article about opposition to mosques in the U.S., chosen at random from Google News

Retirement

My father calls me at least once a week to ask if I know anyone who has ever been abducted by aliens. 'No, I say, I don't.' 'Me neither,' he replies, a hint of regret in his voice.

My father, a life-long agnostic by belief and artist by profession, recently turned eighty. Throughout much of his seventies he was deeply focused on paranormal phenomena and philosophies of reincarnation and the after-life.

At first he read Krishnamurti extensively. Then it was past life regression and out-of-body experiences. Now it is aliens. His chair in the living room is surrounded by books written by mediums, psychics and other experts on the paranormal. Not for him the second adolescence of retirement communities in Boca and the shuffleboard of senior cruises.

His preoccupations remind me of the regimen of religious observances favored in India by the elderly, or those we call 'retirees' and 'senior citizens' in the U.S.

Living in Allahabad some years ago, a combination of climate, gender, friendlessness, foreignness and a dissertation that needed to be written kept me often at home at our rooftop barsaati.

Living in a barsaati affords an excellent view of the courtyards and front yards of neighboring houses. From this vantage point, I could see the neighborhood's senior citizens seated in the sun on their respective charpoys, engaging in religious observances.

In the courtyard of our own house, our landlady, a Partition immigrant from Multan, sat each morning and read small paperback books of Hindu prayers written in Urdu script.

Across the way, a grandfather sat cross-legged on his perch above rows of drying chili peppers, reciting Sanskrit prayers.

Another man, next door, often appeared to be napping or peering over the fence to see what the neighbors were doing, but even he spent a certain amount of time in prayer.

Apprenticeship

Years later, in Chicago, my dissertation on Hindi literature finished, I was determined to learn to read and write Urdu properly, after years of false starts. A colleague helped me find a tutor. He was from the Indian city of Hyderabad, the retired Chair of Arabic Studies at Usmania University. He was also the Sufi imam of a mosque in the basement of the brick courtyard building where he lived on the north side of Chicago, somewhere around the confluence of Clark and Ashland.

As I sat on the floor across from him, reading aloud from Pakistani children's primers, he would nod agreeably and correct me when necessary. All the while he managed from his cell phone the affairs of his flock, fielding calls about problems ranging from the spiritual, to health, to travel, to marital counseling.

As an imam, and an Arabic scholar, my Ustad was, with respect to his spiritual observances, many steps ahead of the retirees I had known in Allahabad. Nevertheless, he was not about to give himself a pass. He took particular care to say the Bismillah in its entirety before undertaking any task, luxuriously elongating the long vowels and stopping to emphasize the consonants: *Bissssmillllaaaah al-Rahmaaaan al-Rahiiiiim.*

It was clear from his delivery that he strove with each invocation to renounce the automatic patter of frequently uttered prayers.

Before beginning anything, whether it was our lesson, or opening the door of my car when I gave him a ride to his son's home, he would stop, shut his eyes and then intone, slowly and loudly: *Bissssmillllaaaah al-Rahmaaaaan al-Rahiiiiim.*

The same practice pertained to sneezing, to which he fell prey in Chicago's allergy season: <sneeze> *Alllhummmmdulllllaaah.*

As his shagird, or student, I was obliged, as much as possible, to help my Ustad, or serve his needs where feasible. This was a perk of which he took only light advantage.

Most often, I gave him rides to various nearby points in his neighborhood, especially in inclement weather. One particular special occasion arose during my time with him.

This was a visit from his son's in-laws, a retired couple who were coming to the U.S. for the first time, having never traveled anywhere besides India and Saudi Arabia. It was arranged that one afternoon I would drive the three of them around the city to see the sights.

Alienation

As we drove up and down various Chicago streets, my Ustad pointed out salient details of the city landscape. After a half an hour or so in the car, we were driving down Clark St., toward Lincoln Park.

Our guests had fallen silent, staring out the windows with that bewilderment one feels in a totally unfamiliar place. At last, scanning the rooftops, the husband remarked thoughtfully, 'You don't see many minarets around here.'

No one wanted to break the news to him that you don't see any minarets in much of the city, so we talked instead of the subtlety of Chicago's mosques, housed unobtrusively in old churches, apartments, storefronts and basements.

Soon we arrived in Lincoln Park, a sprawling green space along the curved shore of Lake Michigan with unobstructed views of the downtown skyline.

Our party made its way slowly along the paths to the shore, dodging joggers, roller-bladers and cyclists. It was a bright spring day, warm enough for Chicagoans to throw off most of their clothing, but slightly chilly for my older Subcontinental companions.

They were all three heavily dressed, the men with turbans, long coats, kurta-pajama, woolen socks and lace-up shoes, the wife of the couple in shalwar-kameez under a long, black robe, her hair covered in a black headscarf.

We sat for some time as they warmed themselves in the sun, mostly in silence, gazing at the lake and people-watching.

After some time, the husband of the couple turned and asked my Ustad with some puzzlement, 'Why do so many people have dogs with them?'

My Ustad did not skip a beat.

'In this country,' he explained, 'everyone is separated: child from parent, husband from wife, brother from sister. They all live alone. They keep these dogs with them as companions in their solitude.'

V.

Rogues Gallery

...if the word 'cowardly' is to be used, it might be more aptly applied to those who kill from beyond the range of retaliation, high in the sky, than to those willing to die themselves in order to kill others. In the matter of courage (a morally neutral virtue): whatever may be said of the perpetrators of Tuesday's slaughter, they were not cowards.

—*Susan Sontag,* The New Yorker *(Sept. 24, 2001)*

Times Square bomber, Faisal Shahzad, in custody.

Green is the theme color in the Shahzads' bedroom. The curtains pick up the tone of the bed linens, and a bamboo print hung between the windows extends the botanical motif.

'There was nothing out of the ordinary about the house,' Del Vecchio [his real estate agent] says. 'There was nothing obvious; no radical posters or anything.'

—From a description of the home of Faisal Shahzad ('The Times Square Bomber') in Connecticut, in CNN Money *((http://bit.ly/blJ6qX))*

When Faisal Shahzad was arrested for trying to detonate a bomb in Times Square, he read out a prepared statement. He spoke of the drone strikes in Pakistan, about the killing of innocents by the U.S. government.

The statement was mostly ignored by the media. Instead we were treated to speculations about how and where he was 'radicalized,' and real estate slideshows of his abandoned, over-mortgaged home in Connecticut:

'Our conversations were plain-vanilla, mostly about the real estate market,' muses his former real estate agent.

Colleen LaRose, aka 'Jihad Jane'.

Pennsylvania native Colleen LaRose was convicted of conspiring to kill Danish cartoonist Lars Vilks.

LaRose 'self-radicalized' online.

The man with whom she was living at the time said she 'never talked about international events, about Muslims, anything.'

Umar Farouk Abdulmutallab, or 'The Underpants Bomber,' trying on a new hat on a school trip to London.

Umar Farouk Abdulmutallab managed to successfully board a flight bound for Detroit from Amsterdam in 2009 equipped with an explosive device wired into his underwear.

*Aafia Siddiqui is known as 'Dr. Aafia' in Pakistan, where she is
'bigger than Jesus,' according to* Chapati Mystery *blogger Sepoy.*

Aafia Siddiqui received a PhD in neuroscience from Brandeis University.

She was later accused of being a courier for al Qaeda. After disappearing for many years, she was apprehended by the CIA and brought to trial in New York. She was convicted of attempting to murder her captors in Afghanistan. She was acquitted of all other charges.

Her case has become a cause célèbre in Pakistan, where she is seen as an innocent victim of a conspiracy on the part of the CIA.

John Walker Lindh, the 'American Taliban'.

John Walker Lindh is the ultimate foreign exchange student.

He left the U.S. to study Arabic and ended up training with al Qaeda in Afghanistan.

His Arabic is reportedly quite good.

Daisy Rockwell

Mohamed Mahmood Alessa with his cat, Tuna Princess.

Mohamed Mahmood Alessa was arrested with his friend (and co-conspirator) on the way to join a militant group in Somalia.

His mother has said that he wanted to take his cat, Tuna Princess, with him, but she did not allow it and they argued. Eventually he left instead with a large bag full of candy from his parents' deli.

The candy was seized by the FBI.

Acknowledgments

None of the writing in this book would ever have happened without the constant encouragement of my co-blogger and friend, Manan Ahmed, aka Sepoy.

The bulk of the writing, and many of the paintings, originally appeared in some form or other on the blog, *Chapati Mystery*, which he generously opened up to me as a writing and exhibition space when I had retreated from academic life in 2006.

Much credit is also due to Amitava Kumar, who has been tremendously supportive along the way.

The book itself would not have been possible without the encouragement of Stephen Marlowe, my beloved editor.

Many thanks are also due to my online community, especially the readers of *Chapati Mystery* and my colleagues on Twitter.

My interest in the material in this book stems in part from my experiences teaching at Loyola University Chicago from 1997-2003, and I owe a debt of gratitude to my students there, who helped inspire me to express myself politically.

I am grateful also for the generous support of my

friends 'in real life,' and to my family, and also Ignatz and Otto, who have been unstinting in their praise of my work.

Most importantly, I must thank my long-suffering husband, without whom nothing is possible, and my daughter, who has taught me to manage my time very effectively.

About the Author

Daisy Rockwell has shown her work in San Francisco, Los Angeles, Philadelphia, North Adams, Massachusetts and White River Junction, Vermont. She paints, and blogs, at *Chapati Mystery* under the pseudonym 'Lapata.'

Rockwell grew up in a family of artists in western Massachusetts, some whose work adorns the surfaces of chinaware and brightens up the waiting rooms of dentists' offices, and others whose artistic output has found more select audiences.

From 1992-2006, she made a detour into Academia, from which she emerged with a PhD in South Asian literature, a book on Upendranath Ashk and a mild case of depression.

CPSIA information can be obtained
at www.ICGtesting.com
Printed in the USA
LVXC01n2124150114
369641LV00015B/58